T0171414

God's House

Eve Rupp

Trafford rev. 09/16/2011

 www.trafford.com

North America & international
toll-free: 1 888 232 4444 (USA & Canada)
phone: 250 383 6864 ♦ fax: 812 355 4082

ACKNOWLEDGMENTS

Computer assistance, Hardware -   Leigh Morrell

Typing, Internet Assistance -   Bobbie Henderson

To my children:

Richard and Barbara

Marjorie

Mary

TABLE OF CONTENTS

CHAPTER 1

"If any of the saints are in need, you must share with them, and make hospitality your special care."
(Rom. 12:13)

They called me from the class I was teaching. The school secretary said, "The hospital called. You should get there as soon as possible." My mother was dying. An hour earlier I had stopped in the hospital chapel and prayed "God, if you're not going to heal her, take her home with You." My prayer had been quickly answered. Another teacher took my place and I headed for the hospital only to learn that my mother died minutes before I got there. I didn't have time to kiss her goodbye - but she wouldn't have known that I was there anyway. She had suffered a massive brain stem hemorrhage nine days earlier and been in a deep coma since the stroke. I prayed, oh how I had prayed, that God would heal her. I wasn't ready to give her up. Even though she was 74 years old, I knew she could live a lot longer. I needed her wisdom and her grandchildren needed their grandmother.

Before I went to school that day, I had stopped at the hospital. They had transferred my mother from intensive care to a regular room and had inserted a nasal - gastric feeding tube. She had vomited the food they had given her through the tube, she inhaled some of it, so each breath gurgled through the food in her lungs. It was all over her face and hair, it covered her pillow and sheets. No one was there to help her.

When I went to ask the nurse for assistance, she said, "Yes, I know your mother needs help, but we have other patients who need help first. I may be able to get to her in about twenty to thirty minutes. No one can come right now." I knew then, that if my mother lived, I would take her home and care for her myself. I wouldn't leave her in such shape. She would receive care when she needed it. Even if she was in a coma, neglecting her needs was not acceptable.

An hour later, after Mom had been cleaned up and again looked as comfortable as possible, I stopped in the hospital chapel to ask God for her release from pain, for the ultimate healing of death. Only death can permanently heal us of the pain and sickness that are so much a part of the human condition. Less than two hours later, she was indeed dead. It was a quick, painful answer to my prayer.

While my mother was around, no one ever went hungry, or naked or sick without her loving help to make life better. I didn't have to worry about where she would spend eternity. She had earned a high place in heaven.

When I grew up, during the big Depression, most mornings there were men, sometimes only one, sometimes five or ten men, sitting on our back steps eating breakfast. My mother always told me, " If someone asks you for food, don't ever turn them away. It could be Jesus you are turning away."

The funeral is a blur in my memory. I don't remember much of what happened or who was there. I know only that there was a Mass and there were friends and strangers present. She was buried beside my father who had died four years before. It was like the earthly center of my life was gone. I moved through each day in a fog.

In the days following the funeral, I began to go through the material accumulation of my Mother's lifetime. Her clothes were washed and given to charity. Some of her furniture was given to relatives who wanted it. There was little that had any value. Both of my parents had always given away more than they kept. Both had been raised in poverty, by widowed mothers, without a father, in the days when the father was the only acceptable breadwinner.

Both used everything until it was completely worn out. My daughter Mary laughed about Grandma's sheets. When bed sheets wore out, she made pillow cases of the least worn sections. When the pillow cases wore out, they were stitched into handkerchiefs for use in bed at night. When the handkerchiefs wore out they were cut up and stitched together to make pen wipers for the fountain pens we used as I was growing up.

Nothing that could be used in any way was ever thrown away, and nothing was purchased until it was needed. If we couldn't use something it was given to someone who could use it. Nothing was kept around that wasn't being used. In later years, their retirement income was small. My father retired early because of his health. Any savings they had were used to put me through college. They lived very simply. While my mother and father lived, no one was ever hungry, or thirsty, or in need when they were around.

My father's uncle stayed with us. During prohibition he made his famous Danish home brew to pay for his keep. During Prohibition that could be a dangerous job. My mother's brother who had been gassed in the first world war, and still suffered the consequences of it, also was a permanent guest in our house. When the abusive man next door threw his wife out of the house with her infant daughter, they too found shelter with us. My dad's brother-in-law died of a heart attack and my aunt moved in. How my mother and dad managed such a household without any rancor or arguing, I will never know. I do know it was a peaceful, happy home, and as children will, I was the only one who disrupted the peace.

After World War II, my aunt married again, so the cantankerous mother of a friend came to stay. She couldn't get along with her daughter. When she left, my diabetic grandmother and paralyzed step-grandfather came when Grandma was no longer able to care for both of them. Then Mom's mother moved in temporarily as she made her rounds of lengthy visits with each of her eight children. She died at our house after only a short stay.

Yes, when I was young, our house was always busy, never empty. I learned well that hospitality was not an option, it was an obligation if you were a follower of Jesus.

As I tried to decide what we should do with her house, I made a thorough inspection. It was built of cypress and pitch pine in 1926. In the 79 years of its existence every surface had been covered with many coats of paint which would have to be removed before a good paint job could be done. The exterior cypress siding showed through where the many coats of paint were peeling off. It hadn't been painted in at least seven years.

The big front porch was a nice welcoming place to sit, but it wasn't screened. In mosquito season we stayed inside. The porch floor was showing signs of rot and would soon need to be replaced.

The front door opened into a small living room with a large brick fireplace that was covered by a gas space heater. There was only room for- about four comfortable chairs and a couple of tables. A sofa would fit if you removed two of the chairs. The dining room was larger and held a small buffet, a china cabinet, an expandable table and six chairs. There were two medium size bedrooms with a bath room that still had the 1926 fixtures: the old tub on legs, the basin with a pedestal. There was no linen closet or storage place for towels and other necessities.

A large, twenty five by fifteen foot family room with ten large windows, had been added at the rear of the house. It too had a fireplace, the only method used to heat old Florida homes. As in the front room, an elderly gas space heater sat in front of the fireplace. It was the only room that boasted a window air conditioner. It was old and wheezed loudly, only half cooling the large room that my mother used as sitting room, and breakfast room. Most of her time was spent there, where she was always busy sewing, knitting or doing other needlework.

In the kitchen, cupboards that went all the way to the nine foot high ceiling, lined the wall over the stove and refrigerator On the other side, high cupboards and a set of drawers flanked a stainless stell sink. The appliances were worn out. A table top water heater sat in one corner. There was no room for a table or chairs, only room to walk between the stove, refrigerator and the sink.

It was an old, comfortable house that needed a lot of work. In its present condition it wouldn't bring much because it would have to go as a "Handy Man's Special". It would require a lot of work before it was really livable regardless of what we decided to do with it.

I didn't want to leave my modern concrete block house with all the modern amenities such as central heat and air conditioning, a dishwasher, a large screened porch, two bathrooms, and a two car garage; so I gave the old house to the Lord, and asked what He wanted done with it. Should we sell it and donate the money to some good cause, or use the money for my children's college education? Maybe He wanted me to donate it to some good organization. What should we do with the house?

We prayed and got no direction, so we prayed some more. "Lord, what shall we do with that house?" We prayed and got no direction, so we prayed some more. "Lord what shall we do with that house?" In the meantime we had begun to make some of the repairs that would be necessary regardless of our decision. Finally, after eight months of asking, both my husband and I knew that the Lord had accepted the house as His own. It needed caretakers. We knew that we were to move in and take any one that He sent to us and welcome them as we would welcome the Lord. It was an overwhelming idea. How would we know if these strangers were safe to take into our house? Maybe we imagined the whole idea.

We talked to our pastor, Father David, about it. He thought it would be wonderful to have a place like that for emergency shelter, but he really couldn't advise us to take such a step. We talked to the leaders of our prayer group, but they were no more helpful than Father David. Three scriptures kept coming to mind: The first was Isaiah 56: 6-7 "And the strangers who join themselves to the Lord, these I will bring to my holy mountain, and make them joyful in my house of prayer. For my house shall be called a house of prayer for all peoples." The second was Romans 12:13, "If any of the saints are in need, you must share with them. You must make hospitality your special care." The most important was Hebrews 13:2 "Do not neglect Hospitality to strangers, for through it some have unknowingly entertained angels."

After much discussion, we decided that we should act in obedience to what we thought was God's direction for us by moving into God's House and put our new house up for sale. If the idea was from God we wouldn't have to look or advertise. People would find their way to us without any action on our part. If the idea was from God, we would sell our other house quickly and could use the money from the sale to make necessary repairs. If the idea was not from God, no one would come to our house to stay, and the improvements would either make the house more livable so we would want to stay, or make it more valuable to sell. Either way, we felt that our interests were covered.

As it was January when we moved in, the first repair we made was to install a gas wall furnace that would heat all the rooms in the main part of the house. Then we had the chimneys and fireplaces repaired and checked so we could build a fire and sit in front of it enjoying the beauty and the warmth. We rented a sandblaster, and paid our son to sandblast the exterior walls, remove all the peeling paint and finish the beautiful cypress wood with a wood preservative and a stain, so the siding looks like driftwood. We replaced the clogged sewer line, and the leaky water pipes. The electric service was woefully inadequate, and needed repair and modernizing to current code standards. We did that as soon as possible.

As we began on the inside of the house, we found that we also had a problem with peeling paint on the walls of the front bedroom. We scraped as much as we could and covered the rest with paneling. In the living room we papered the wall opposite the fireplace and painted the rest of the interior in light, cheerful yellow. White woodwork and drapes against dark green walls made the huge back room look more comfortable. We took one corner of the large room and installed a bathroom and large linen closet. When the hot water heater failed, we put the new one outside next to the house and installed a dishwasher where the old water heater had been. Slowly we organized what was left of our furniture and my mother's Furniture. God's House became a comfortable home.

By shutting the door between the middle bedroom and the back room, there was a small apartment, complete except for a kitchen. There was the small bedroom, the new bath and the large sitting area. I kept the corner next to the bathroom as a sewing/art room for my own use. When our guests came, they could stay at the back of the house with privacy for them and for us. God's House was ready for its first guests.

We developed a list of rules that would be a guide for anyone staying with us. Many of the rules are scripture based and have served well for over 20 years. They applied to my husband and I as well as to our guests.

Colossians, 3:12-17 "You are God's chosen race, His saints; He loves you, and you should be clothed in sincere compassion, in kindness and humility, gentleness and patience. Bear with one another; forgive each other as soon as a quarrel begins. The Lord has forgiven you; now you must do the same. Over all these clothes, to keep them together and complete them, put on love. And may the Peace of Christ reign in your hearts, because it was for this that you were called together as parts of one body. Always be thankful. Let the message of Christ and all its richness find a home with you. Teach each other and advise each other in all wisdom".

I Timothy 3:4 "He must be a man who manages his own family well and brings his children up to obey him and to be well behaved." Dick is head of the house and is to be consulted about any matters that affect the household. When Dick is absent, Eve will handle any concerns. When neither is present, in serious matters consult the pastor of our church.

II Thessalonians 3:10 "We gave you a rule when we were with you; not to let anyone have any food if he refused to do any work." Guests are responsible for cleaning the rooms they occupy including the bathroom. Clean linen is available. We will provide rags, a vacuum, and cleaning supplies.

Philippians 4:8 "Fill your minds with everything that is true, everything that is noble, everything that is good and pure, everything that we love and honor, and everything that can be thought virtuous or worthy of praise." All witchcraft, magic sorcery, astrology, pornography, violence, horror stories, etc., in books, printed materials or on TV, do not belong in this house.

Any guests you entertain are to leave by 9:00 pm. No smoking in the house. All smoking materials and matches are only to be used outside the house, on the back or front porch. The phone may be used for local calls only. If in an emergency you must make a long distance call, be sure to reverse the charges. No calls are to be over 10 minutes in length, as we have incoming calls that need to be answered. When you leave the house, please tell us you are leaving, and when we can expect you back. We will give you the same courtesy. We need to know if you will be present for meals. Each guest is a gift from God. May your stay here be pleasant and peaceful; may it bless your life as it will bless ours.

CHAPTER 2

God's Provision is Always an Abundance

"Seek first the Kingdom of God and His righteousness,
and all these things will be given to you as well."
(Mat. 6:33)

All things that we really needed were provided for our house, either as gifts or with the money needed in good bargains. We always prayed for what we needed, and one way or another it was always provided. Two outstanding provisions of our needs are described in this chapter. There were many provisions, not all as plain as these.

I was working as a teacher, which requires a lot of time outside the classroom. One Saturday I was sitting on the living room floor, sewing together the braids that had come loose from my mother's hand braided rug. I had other concerns; paper grading, materials to collect for Monday's classes, as well as the rest of the house to clean, and dinner to prepare. I spoke to the Lord with some impatience. "Lord, I have better things to do than sit here and mend these darn rugs. I really need wall-to-wall carpeting. These floors are worn and discolored they need to be covered. Where will I get the money for them? You know where our money goes. What can I do about it?" I went on with the mending and didn't think of them again.

On Monday morning the phone rang, and a friend of ours, who owned a flooring store said, "Eve, did you want some rugs?" I said, "Yes, what do you have?" "Well", he said, "Some carpets in a local condominium, got partly wet, and have to be replaced. The insurance company wants to regain part of their loss. They want to sell the rest." "How much" I asked. "Oh, offer them 80 dollars." he answered. "Eighty dollars we could afford, "We'll take it." I answered. He said, "It'll need padding, without it, it will wear out sooner and not be as comfortable." "How much?" I asked. "About twice what you will pay for the rugs," he answered. "Sorry," I said, "That we can't afford." "Well, I understand, but it won't be as good."

When they delivered the rugs, it was as though the Lord had measured our two rooms and gave us just what we needed, with little left over. The gold color also went very well with our pale yellow walls. We laid the carpet and it was exactly what we needed. The next day when I went to school, one of the other teachers came into the break room carrying a stack of rug padding sample squares. She said, "Someone gave us a whole car load of these. Does anyone have a use for them? " "I do," I said. I took them home, used duct tape to put them together and had the rug padding I needed.

Another example of God's generous answer to our need was the fact that my husband needed a different car. He worked at Disney World as an animation technician and drove fifty miles a day to and from his job. The ten-year-old car we had, was constantly breaking down in spite of Dick's talent with mechanics. It was obvious we needed a different car before ours broke down permanently. We were, as usual, without enough savings to buy a new car so we had an insurance policy that had covered our children when they were at home. It was worth $1800, not enough to purchase a new car, but enough for a good down payment.

We joined hands and prayed before we left to find a car. We asked for a car, in good condition that required as little gas for the fifty-mile daily drive as possible. The first two car lots we stopped at had nothing like what we needed. All the cars were either worn out or cost too much.

At the third lot, I stayed in the car and prayed for a good bargain when Dick came banging on the window, saying excitedly, "COME HERE, come here, look at what I've found". I got out of the car with him and there was a bright red MG midget convertible. It had 7 miles on it, was three years old, and just happened to cost $1800. Always the doubter about such good luck, I asked why it was so cheap. The salesman answered, "Well, the car body was damaged taking it off the boat. It had been in litigation to determine who was responsible and who would repair it and who would pay for it. It has been repaired and we just want to get what we could out of it. You were the first ones who were interested in it." God's hand was clearly seen in the deal.

The car served us well for about five years. We even drove it to Ohio, where our extended family lived, and back to Orlando, before we sold it and looked for another car. What God provides is always perfect for us.

CHAPTER 3

God Heals In Many Ways

"My child, when you are ill, do not be depressed, but pray to the Lord and He will heal you. "
(Sirach 38: 9-14)

At my yearly physical, the doctor found several large lumps in my right breast, which had been small lumps only six months earlier. He told me that the rate of growth and other characteristics indicated that it was probably cancerous. He advised that I should have surgery as soon as possible. Frightened, I agreed with him. It would be a week before the surgeon, the operating room, more x-rays, and other details could be coordinated. Surgery was set for a week and a half from that day.

I was devastated. Cancer at that time in the late 70's, early 80's was almost always a death sentence. The first place I turned for help was scripture. I just opened the book and it opened to Sirach, a book from the Catholic Bible. Sirach 38: 9-14 were words that seemed to be written just for me.

"My son, when you are ill, delay not, but pray to God who will heal you. Flee wickedness, let your hands be just, cleanse your heart of every sin. Offer your sweet smelling oblation and petition, a rich offering according to your means. Then give the doctor his place, lest he leave, for you need him too.

There are times that give him an advantage and he too beseeches God that his diagnosis may be correct and his treatment bring about a cure".

I believed that God had spoken to me though his scriptures. I went to confession to cleanse my heart of all sin, and wrote the largest check we could afford to the church. As instructed, my husband and I prayed for healing every evening and when we went to prayer meetings everyone prayed for me. I was at peace – all fear was gone. I was ready for surgery. As I was wheeled into the room for that surgery, there was a hymn of praise playing in my head.

Afterward when I woke up from the anesthetic the doctor came in and said, "I really don't understand it. Even after I got the tumor out, it had every appearance of malignancy. But when it was examined microscopically, no cancer cells could be found." There were no cancer cells in it, I had been healed, bless the Lord who cares so well for His children.

CHAPTER 4

Two Women From Columbia

"My house shall be a house of prayer for all peoples"
(Isaiah 56:7)

Padre Domingo was all upset. His voice over the phone betrayed his distress because his Cuban accent got heavier. He also had more difficulty finding the right English word. "What am I to do with them?" he asked. "Two women and two small children - they have too little English. I have no place to put them! It is Saturday night and I have no money for a motel. They cannot stay in the rectory. What am I to do with them? They cannot stay on the street. They are cultured ladies, not the kind that sleep in the gutter!"

I calmed him as best I could and asked who told him to call our house? "Juan Martinez from your prayer group said you might have a place for them to sleep. I had to call you. I had nothing else I could do" he answered.

I remembered, at our last prayer meeting we had asked for prayer for guidance about whether we heard the Lord correctly when we thought he asked us to open our home. Maybe this was the answer to our prayers. At least we would try. Dick went down to the rectory to pick them up. If they had little English, I was worse off because I had almost no Spanish. While awaiting their arrival, I made up the twin beds in the back bedroom for the ladies, a pull out couch for the children in case they were young enough to share a bed, and cushions on the floor for one if they weren't. I had no idea of their ages. I put a pot of coffee on. If they were from Columbia as Father Domingo said then maybe they would like a drink of their national beverage when they arrived.

When the car pulled in the drive, I went to greet our very first guests, and used what little Spanish I had when I told them, "Mi casa - Su Casa ". I hoped it meant what I thought. I wasn't sure. I hoped I had said, "My house is your house." Evidently it must have been close because they were delighted and relieved by the greeting.

After the children were put to bed, we talked to the ladies. Over a cup of coffee we learned that Dolores, the older woman, spoke no English. I suspected she understood more than she let us know. Maria had learned a good deal of English from watching television and we were able to understand each other quite well. Maria was Dolores' daughter-in-law.

Maria and Fernando had come from Columbia with their children to improve their way of life. Fernando, Maria's husband, had been a bookkeeper for one of the large hotels on International Drive until he was arrested and convicted of armed robbery and attempted murder of a shopkeeper. He was awaiting his sentence hearing in the Orange County Jail.

Dolores had come from Columbia to be with her family in this time of need. They were sending the children by air back to Columbia the next day to stay with other family members during this difficult time. The plane tickets had taken the rest of their money. They could not pay their rent and they had sold their furniture to help pay the plane fare. Neither woman had a job, they had been forcibly evicted from their apartment earlier in the day. They turned to the only sanctuary they knew, they turned to the church.

They left early the next morning to take the children to the airport and began the search for jobs. They were both hired as maids in one of the hotels. At least they would earn enough to pay for gas for their old car, some legal necessities such as court transcripts for the appeal, and to send a little back to Columbia to help support their children. The family property in Columbia had already been heavily mortgaged to pay legal costs and get money for an appeal.

They looked for a lawyer to handle an appeal on the grounds that their defense attorney was incompetent. They hired one who was best known for defending famous criminal cases but they had no way of judging his competence nor his honesty. He told me the man was guilty, that was all that he needed to know. He took their money and never did a thing to start the appeal process. He got what he wanted and cared nothing for what happened to them. I didn't realize how great was the injustice until I read the trial transcript. It was a serious case of injustice against a foreigner. The crime took place in early December during rush hour at 5:25 pm. at a photo shop north of downtown Orlando. The robber shot the store owner grazing the side of his head with the bullet but the wound was not serious enough to even make him unconscious. The owner's original description of the robber was of a man five foot ten inches to six foot tall with no accent. Fernando was arrested in late June and charged with the crime. The photo shop owner picked him out of a line-up and said that he was the man who shot him. Fernando had been in the shop several times to purchase photo supplies, so would naturally look familiar to the shop owner. He was only five foot two inches tall and could barely speak understandable English because of his thick accent. Yet he was arrested and convicted because he "acted guilty."

Maria told me that when he was arrested they had no idea what they had been doing at that time over six months earlier. They searched their calendar, their checkbook and bank-records. They found that there had been a celebration that afternoon at the hotel for someone who had been promoted. About fifteen people had been present and had talked to Maria and Fernando. The party ended less than ten minutes before the robbery took place fifteen miles away through rush hour traffic on some of the busiest roads in Orange County. Several people testified that Maria and Fernando had stayed until the party was over.

Maria and Fernando had asked for a court translator because in the pressure of the courtroom it was hard to think in English. The judge said both Maria and Fernando spoke English well enough and didn't need a translator. The trial was conducted entirely in English and the lawyer did not even protest any of these injustices.

I spoke to a person who had been present at the trial and she said, "Oh, he acted so guilty." The question is, were his "guilty" actions prompted by guilt or by fear of the unknown and ignorance of exactly what was happening in the courtroom? The jury pronounced him guilty. It seemed as though they probably did have cause for an appeal, if they could find a good lawyer.

The gift of tongues works in many ways. Dolores would speak to me in Spanish and I would speak in English, but somehow we managed to understand each other. We would get peculiar glances from people in stores who would overhear our bilingual conversation. Somehow it worked.

We prayed together nightly for Fernando's freedom, help with the appeal, and strength for the two women who were trying to manage the appeal, work responsibilities, and separation from their children. Their faith and patience during all these difficulties were powerful lessons for us about the power of faith in God. We learned more from them about trusting in God than we could possibly have taught them. During one of our prayer sessions I "saw" in my mind things blowing away tumbling in a strong wind. Then in the midst of the chaos there appeared a large cross. Anyone who caught the cross didn't get blown away but became part of the cross - for the cross was made up not of wood or stone but was made up of people. What I understood from those mental images was that community was the cross and the cross was community. Only when we became one in charity and prayer would we be safe from the violent "winds" that were blowing through our society. As we tried to establish God's House, we were becoming part of the cross, part of Jesus' work of salvation.

When Fernando received his sentence, it was a black day for them. He received a sentence of eighty years. He was to be transferred to Lake Butler Reception Center within a month. Maria wept loudly, "How can my children grow up without their father? How can I live without my husband? I will be dead before he is released. I have been sentenced with him!" We comforted her as best we could.

The appeal lawyer they hired was not much help and always demanded more money. Their small salary as maids in a hotel didn't go very far. There was no evidence of an appeal hearing or any action toward a just outcome for the situation. The lawyer in reality did nothing and when I protested said, "Oh, he probably is guilty anyway." Things were not hopeful, but they trusted that God would pull them through.

Fernando was transferred to Lake Butler Corrections Reception Center, where they could only visit him once a month. His photography skills were to be used in photographing new arrivals before they were transferred to other penitentiaries. He would remain at the Lake Butler Facility. There was no sign of the appeal hearing they needed and had paid an exorbitant amount to obtain. All available money was gone and they had no other choice but to return to Columbia.

I saw them again when they came to our house about a year later. Working with the Colombian embassy and a lawyer the embassy helped them find, they were applying to have Fernando deported from the U.S. as an undesirable alien. The appeal worked and the family was reunited in Columbia. Once again they could be a family and live a normal life because there were no charges against Fernando in his own country. The only results of the injustice were two years lost to the trial and imprisonment and permanent exile from the United States.

From our first guests we learned many things. Among them, God is always there to support us through all our troubles; God corrects injustices, but usually does not work as fast as we would like; and differences in language and in culture are not a barrier to the working of the community of faith. Maria and Delores suffered much during their time with us. The suffering increased their faith not decrease it. Because of their faith and their patience, the Lord reunited their family.

CHAPTER 5

Journey From Death Into Eternal Life

"But it was only right we should celebrate and rejoice, because your brother here was dead and has come to life, he was lost and is found."

(Luke 15:32)

It had been a good prayer meeting at the Cathedral. The prayer and praise flowed naturally; the presence of God was very strong. There was much to think about that evening. As my husband and I walked out across the patio Father David called to us, "Eve, Dick, how's your spare room?" I told him it was empty. He said, "This is Joe. It seems he had decided to kill himself but thought maybe he might give life a second chance so he came to see me. We've been talking but it's late now and he needs a place to stay. Take him home with you until he gets things straightened out."

I really looked at Joe for the first time. He stood over six feet tall and seemed all arms and legs, obviously an unfinished adolescent. The sleeves of his jacket ended about four inches above his wrists and his trousers ended a good six inches above his shoes. He had thick straight black hair that hadn't been combed in a while and poked out in all directions. The beautiful part of his face were those liquid brown eyes that showed a terrible amount of hurt.

I asked if he had any baggage to take with him. "No" he said, "I didn't think I'd need anything. Everything's at my sister's." I asked him if he was going back to his sister's house tomorrow? He responded, "She said I couldn't come back, ever". "Can we get your clothes and other things tomorrow?" I asked. "Yeah, I guess so, if she didn't throw everything away when she beat me up with the broom handle and threw me out." "Can we call her tomorrow? Do you know her phone number?" I asked "Yeah, but she won't talk to me. She might talk to you, though", he said hopefully. "Well we'll find that out tomorrow. Tonight we have to go home and get a good night's sleep. Have you had anything to eat?" "Not today. I did have something yesterday at Our Daily Bread." "First you've got to eat, then a good night's sleep will make everything look better."

He talked as I fixed him supper, and he ate. I learned that he was 15, "almost 16", that his mother, an alcoholic, died when he was seven, and his father, also an alcoholic abandoned Joe and his baby sister. They had lived in the worst part of the Chicago slums. Stealing and other crimes were his only means of survival when his mother and father were drunk. As though he were daring me to make something of it he said, "I'm a liar and a thief". "That's only what you are if that's what you want to be. You can decide to be anything you want." I told him.

He went on with his sad story. Chicago social workers put him in a boy's home for a while. When he was there he was sexually abused by the older boys and decided that he was probably a homosexual.

His older half-brother, an ex-Marine, found out that he could collect Social Security for him if he took custody of him. He started to discipline him with the worst kind of military discipline, including holding him under steaming showers and then under icy showers. He had to stand at attention for long hours and was beaten if he relaxed. He had to go without food as punishment many times. Chicago social services decided the treatment he was getting was abusive and placed him in an Episcopal boy's home. There, the older boys also sexually abused him. After a few years of that his older half-sister took custody of him and brought him to Florida. She was unable to handle him, and started to beat him. That was when he decided to run away and kill himself. Not really ready to end his life, he turned to Father David for help.

The next day I called his sister who, only too glad to be rid of him, offered to bring his clothes over. He had no other possessions. I looked at the clothes and none of them would fit him. He must have gone through a recent growth spurt, as fifteen-year-old boys will, and outgrew everything he owned. His sister bought him nothing new. I called Father David and told him that our budget that month didn't allow for a new wardrobe for a fifteen-year-old boy. He told me to come to the rectory and gave me enough to buy the necessities.

We talked about school and he said he had dropped out in seventh grade. Joe wasn't eager to return to school. He had never done well in school, "I'm just a dummy, I guess." and he wanted to be on his own. I asked how he would earn his living. He hadn't thought that far ahead. Reluctantly he agreed that maybe school would be the best thing for him. He would see what it was like. With his size, and his low academic achievement level, I figured he didn't belong in either high school or junior high. I really didn't know where Joe would fit in society. Maybe a stable home life would enable him to blossom and learn. He seemed to have a great deal of untutored intelligence if only it could be developed. I talked about the GED program where you could begin with whatever you knew and learn what was necessary to get the equivalent of a high school diploma. I told him the teachers gave a lot of personal instruction and a Graduate Equivalency Diploma would help him get a job later. Reluctantly he agreed to try the class because he would like to graduate from high school.

With the permission of his sister we took legal custody of Joe and made arrangements for his Social Security to come to us. We took a small amount out to help pay for food and other necessities including a weekly allowance for him. A fifteen-year-old boy can eat a huge amount each day and he rapidly outgrew all clothes. I put the rest in an account that required both his and my signatures to remove it. I figured when he left us it would give him a way to begin a new life.

Dick, my husband, was working with the convert classes at our church and Joe was interested. The first religious instruction he received had been at the Episcopal Boys Home where he had been baptized. He wanted to know more. He decided he wanted to go with Dick and become a Catholic. He attended classes regularly and was confirmed on that Easter Sunday.

His school attendance and work were very inconsistent. Some days he would breeze right through, then other days it was as though he was lost. He had no idea where to even begin with his studies. When I would call the school to learn how he was doing I was told that he had been absent at least half the time. He struggled through for about six months when he said that he didn't understand the work with the teacher he had, so we transferred him to another school. The results were no different.

I took Joe for psychiatric counseling at the Christian Service Center. When the counselor began to probe too close to the truth Joe refused to go anymore. He was unable to accept what he was doing with his life and his probable homosexuality, or where his unwise choices would take him.

I talked about Joe's lack of responsibility to a priest friend who had worked in the neighborhood where Joe grew up. That's where I learned that if anyone from that neighborhood succeeded it was a miracle. Not only was he from a bad environment but his alcoholic parents and the time he had spent in an institution also worked against him. My friend said that in his experience children who were mainly raised in institutions suffered from what he called "institution syndrome." They had never been allowed to take responsibility for their own choices and actions but were always told what to do and when to do it. They never developed a sense of responsibility. He had no suggestions about what to do for Joe, as far as his experience went, there was no cure. In today's schools he would probably be diagnosed as suffering from Attention Deficit Disorder, or Fetal Alcohol Syndrome, probably both.

Paying attention to any one thing for longer than five minutes seemed impossible. Since he wouldn't or couldn't take school seriously, we talked to him about finding a job. He was hired in a fast food restaurant as bus boy and dishwasher. He treated the job as he had treated the school. His employment lasted for about one week.

Joe did enjoy working in the yard if he could do what he wanted there. Taking an assigned task and completing it seemed to be beyond his capabilities. He liked to build things in the yard and he liked to plant things. A three-foot cherry laurel tree that he planted in our front yard is now over 25 feet tall. If only there had been someone who could work beside him until he learned to complete the task at hand, maybe he would have learned. With both my husband and I employed, no one really had the time.

On his eighteenth birthday we celebrated his legal "coming of age". He was again trying to work on finishing his schooling. On the day after his birthday he didn't come home. I called the school and was told that he hadn't been there for more than a week. I called the police. When the detective came to the house, I told him that I knew I was no longer responsible for Joe, he was by law an adult - but I was worried and wondered where he was. The detective made a few phone calls, and said, "Well I've found him. He's in Orange County Jail. He stole a bathing suit yesterday at the Mall near the school and got himself arrested. His bail is set at seventy-five dollars. If you want you can bail him out or leave him there. It's up to you." I took the seventy-five dollars out of his funds and bailed him out of jail.

"Joe, why did you do it," I asked." Because I just wanted to find out if I still could get away with it," he answered. "Now you know it's not a good idea. Things like lying and theft will always bring trouble that you don't need. Unless you want to spend most of the rest of your life in jail, you need to decide right now that the part of your life where you lived by theft is over. You need to make a new beginning."

At his court date a couple of weeks later, he pleaded "no contest" to the charges and was fined two hundred fifty dollars, which took the rest of the money I had saved for him. My husband and I decided that it was time to lay down the law. We were going on vacation and invited him to go with us but when we came back he would have to choose one of three options: he could settle down and finish school with no more absences; he could settle down, get a job and pay rent; or he could find another place to live. He decided not to go with us. He said he wanted to think about what he should do. That was agreeable to us so we said we'd see him in ten days.

When we returned home Joe was nowhere to be found. His room was a disaster area with most of his few belongings scattered everywhere mixed in with dirty dishes, candy, fast food wrappers, and just junk that he had picked up here and there. The dresser drawers were pulled out half empty and laying on the floor. He had taken a piece of my jewelry to pawn, a hunting knife of my husband's, and a sleeping bag. He was traveling light, taking only a few of his clothes and leaving everything else. He left a note thanking us for letting him stay with us but he had decided to make it on his own.

We heard nothing from him for almost a year, then one day he showed up on our front porch. He asked to come back and live with us again, that he would get a job and pay rent. We said no. From the beginning my husband and I had agreed that after someone left our house they couldn't come back again. If the person hadn't learned what they needed to know the first time it was unlikely they would learn what was needed the second time. We had no revolving door. Father David was very upset with our decision and asked us to change our minds and let him come back. My husband absolutely refused. He said, "He has decided that it's OK to steal from us. Nothing will be safe if we allow him to come back. He has to learn that his bad choices have consequences." I knew he was right. Even though I had a hard time refusing, we turned him away.

About a month later we heard that he had gotten a job on a ranch in St. Cloud, a small city south of Orlando. It seemed that such a job was probably just what he needed, and he was on his way to independence. We heard no more.

About 12 years later, just before Christmas, Joe called from Los Angeles. "Mom", he said, "I've been awful bad. I've been living with this guy - letting him support me and use me. I've been going with this older woman and sleeping with her when she wants. I've lied to everybody and taken what I wanted. I want out but I don't know how to get out. I don't like what I've become." I told him to go to the nearest Catholic Church and tell the priest there just what he had told me. The priest would help him find the help he needed. I assured him that God always loved him, and would forgive him as soon as he turned to God and asked for forgiveness. I also said that the way of life he had chosen didn't bring happiness. He needed to change his choices so he could be happy. We then talked about other things, what our family had been doing and what his friends in Orlando were doing. He said he'd look for that priest and hung up.

Shortly after the first of the year, I got a call from his younger sister who lived in St. Cloud. The police had called her from Los Angeles. Joe had gotten drunk and on his way home one of the local gangs had beaten him and thrown him off a five-story building. He was brain dead. The police wanted his two sisters to come out to Los Angeles and sign permission to turn off the life support machines but they had no money for the trip. I called Father David and he helped them get their tickets. I talked to them and asked that they call a priest to anoint him before they turned off the life support as he had chosen to be a Catholic. They said they would and left for California.

When they returned I received a large envelope in the mail from his younger sister. It contained a photograph of Joe that he had used when he applied for acting jobs as an extra in Hollywood. He had been a very handsome young man. In a letter she told how the priest had come and prayed with Joe before they turned off the life support. She said the prayers and the assurance of God's love made his death easier for them to take. How can we look at the life of a young man such as Joe? He made so many wrong decisions in his life. Did he ever really have a chance at a good moral life? I don't know. I do believe however, that when he called me just before Christmas, he really repented of the wrong he had done and God took him home before he could change his mind. I expect to meet him again some day after I go home to God.

CHAPTER 6

Deception Can Be A Way of Life

"Then Jesus began to tell them, Take care that no one deceives you."

(Mark 13:5)

My friend, Elizabeth, called and said, "Eve, there was a young woman sitting in church after Mass this morning crying as though her heart would break. When I tried to comfort her she told me that she was about to be put out on the streets - she is being evicted from her furnished room downtown and has no place to go. I gave her your name and number hoping you would be able to help her. Her name is Alice. She will probably be calling you."

I asked, "Why is she being evicted? No one gets evicted without reason."

"Well," Elizabeth said, "It seems she was sharing a room with another young woman and they had a fight. She is working. She's a nurse's aid at Lucerne Hospital. She spent all her money on the month's rent for the room and buying groceries. The other woman told some terrible lies about her and the landlord said she would have to move. She doesn't have any money until she gets paid the end of the month so she has nowhere else to go. She'll be able to get her own place the end of the month. She only needs a place for two weeks." "I'll talk to her, that's all I can promise at this point" I told her. "I'll let you know what happens."

The call from Alice came later that afternoon. "A lovely lady gave me your phone number this morning in St. James Church and said that maybe you could help me." I asked, "Just what kind of help do you need?" "I'm being evicted from my room. I just need a place to stay for a couple of weeks until I get my next paycheck and can find another room to rent. Do you rent rooms? Could I stay with you?" "We provide emergency shelter for people who have no where else to go on a short time basis. If you have the money and want to pay twenty-five dollars a week for your food, laundry and electricity, we will accept that. The room is free. If you are interested, come over this afternoon and we'll talk."

Alice arrived later that afternoon. She told of the argument with her roommate and the reasons she had to leave. Then she said that she had testified in a drug trial in Texas and was in the witness protection plan. A drug cartel leader had marked her for execution, so she would need a place where not many people knew where she was. Of course "Alice" was not her real name. She wouldn't or couldn't give us her real name. No she couldn't give us her parent's phone number for emergency use only. Her parent's phone was probably bugged.

She would, however give us the name and phone extension number of a detective with the local police department who was her contact. If necessary, he would contact her parents. If she stayed with us, we must not under any condition tell any one about her presence.

As she talked, the thought came into my mind, "She's acting. None of it is true!" My conscience reminded me that we must not judge any one. How uncharitable I was to doubt the poor girl's story. Only later would I learn to recognize and use the gift of the Holy Spirit called "the gift of discernment". This gift allows us to recognize and tell the difference between good and evil. It was too bad that I didn't pay attention to it that day.

She moved her few things into our back bedroom the next day, saying, "Oh, what a relief! You have no idea how wonderful it is to feel safe again! Thank you, thank you for taking me in." She said her health was not good and she couldn't always get to work because she suffered from endometriosis that caused a lot of pain during her monthly periods, so if she didn't get up for work I wasn't to think it strange. She said her father suffered from Lou Gehrig's disease and the greatest sorrow of her life was that she couldn't be with him during his final days. They had a special phone number that only she could use so that she could check on his progress regularly. She assured me that all those long distance calls would be reversed charges.

Alice started getting strange phone calls that apparently frightened her. "They've found where I am" she said, her eyes wide as though in fear. "That's ridiculous," I told her. "How could they possibly get this number? What did they say to you?" "They didn't say anything. There was just heavy breathing on the line." "How do you know it's someone who is your enemy if they didn't say anything?" I asked.

The calls would come several times a day, but only when Alice was home from work. I began to worry. Were we in danger from Alice's enemies? When I prayed about the situation, there was just peace, no fear, about what we were doing.

Strange letters started to arrive in the mail. She showed me one of them. It was unsigned, typewritten, and said her days were numbered; they would get her wherever she was. I told her to give it to the detective that was her contact, that they could trace a type written letter because all typewriters are unique. There are small variations in the letters that allow detectives to prove that a letter came from a specific typewriter.

No more typewritten letters arrived, instead letters addressed with letters cut from a magazine began arriving. The strange phone calls increased, as did the frequency of the letters. She had many appointments with her "contact", the detective, to assure that the drug dealers she had testified against were not active in this area. She seemed to be constantly frightened. She said the F.B.I. was investigating the threatening letters.

I learned from a visit to Lucerne Hospital that, yes, she did work there; but, no, she wasn't a nurse's aid, she was a custodial worker. One morning, about two weeks later, I went to the kitchen to put out the trash for pickup, and it was gone. I thought it was very strange as I was usually the one who did that chore. My husband left for work at Disney by 5:30 am. and had no time for such things. I went to look and sure enough the bags were neatly tied in knots, not with a wire twist as Dick or I would tie them, and resting at the curb. I wondered, what is so important in that trash that she had to carry it out herself? I brought the bags up on the porch, opened them and began to examine their contents. The first thing I found was a magazine that had words cut out of it. Looking further, I found many magazines that were the source of all the "threatening" letters supposedly sent to Alice. I knew then, she was the source of the threatening letters and the phone calls were faked. The words of the Spirit on the day I first talked to her were correct. She was acting; nothing about her stories was true.

I called the detective who she said was her contact and told him what I had found. He thanked me and said he would be right over. He said that The F.B.I. had indeed been investigating the "threatening" letters she was receiving, and they would be glad to learn the real source of those letters. There was no threat to public safety. The trial and legal contacts that she was so busy taking care of were in reality the prosecution of a panhandler from downtown Orlando who had annoyed her. The detective knew nothing of any witness program, or drug dealer connection with her. He said that the letters were a Federal offense, and the police department would not press charges if she got some mental health treatment. Obviously she was badly in need of such help He took the cut-up magazines with him to the Police Department.

When she came home from work, she confronted me; "How DARE you open my trash bags! That is an invasion of MY privacy! You had no right to touch them after I put them out at the curb! They were MY bags, and what was in them was MY information."

"Alice, you lied to us, to all of us. Why did you do such a thing?"

She shouted, "You deserved to be lied to! How eager you were to believe all I told you. How stupid you were to swallow those stories."

I told her, "You can no longer stay here. If you remember, the rules you read quoted Paul's letter to the Philippians, "Fill your minds with everything that is true. You are to have all your possessions out of this house before supper."

"I'm going right now - I don't want to stay here another minute." She disappeared into the back room and came out a few minutes later with her suitcases. Without another word, she was out the front door, slamming it behind her.

A few months later Father David told us that Alice had asked to be married in the church to a sailor from the Naval Training Center. He said that she couldn't or wouldn't produce the proper documents, Baptismal certificate, or birth certificate, so he couldn't marry them. I reminded him of Alice's untruthfulness.

Two weeks later he said that he heard from Alice's husband. A justice of the peace had married them. He got up one morning and she was gone. There was no note, no explanation, she just left. He was heartbroken as he felt that God had given her to him so he could protect her. He had gone to the police who already knew all about her. They told him that she had left town.

The Apostle John tells us in his gospel, *"But when He comes, the Spirit of Truth, He will guide you to all truth."* (John 16:13) If we only take the time to pray and ask for truth, then listen for the answers, we will save ourselves many sorrows. We received the Holy Spirit in Baptism and at Confirmation, yet how little most of us listen to the One who will guide us to all truth. That was the hard lesson we learned from Alice's stay with us. Knowledge of the truth is there for us. All we need to do is ask and listen.

Another hard lesson we learned from Alice's visit was that sympathetic friends are not objective enough to safely recommend people for our house. Perhaps God did send Alice to us because He is always giving each of us a chance to change the choices that make us unhappy.

We seriously considered changing our procedures for inviting people to stay with us. We decided that only if a religious professional or a social worker sent them and had evaluated their need, their truthfulness, and recommended that we help them, could we permit them to stay.

CHAPTER 7

A Journey from Evil into Baptism and the Kingdom of God

"But if it is through the Spirit of God that I cast out devils then know that the Kingdom of God has overtaken you"

(Matthew 12:28)

The call came from the catechist who was responsible for teaching new converts at the Catholic Cathedral, a good friend of ours, named Roy. He was an excellent teacher and theologian. He said, "Eve, how is your spare room?"

"At present it's empty, but if you ask, I imagine it won't stay that way long".

"We have a young woman, named Patricia, who wants to be baptized. She was involved in spiritualism, drugs and other assorted evils. She has all the symptoms of demonic oppression, not possession, because she still has the use of her free will. At present she is being pushed toward suicide because she wants Baptism. She has a real spiritual battle on her hands. She lives alone and I'm afraid that if she doesn't have a good Christian family to support her through this period of learning, she'll never live to be baptized. She is seeing a psychiatric counselor at Catholic Social Services, but she needs more support than they can give her. Can she stay with you for the next nine months until she is ready for Baptism at Easter?"

I really didn't understand what I was getting into, but I said. "Let me talk it over with Dick first, but I'm sure she can stay with us. We'll be glad to support her through the instruction period. If Dick says no, I'll call you right back. If you don't hear from me, it's all right."

Patricia came over, we talked, and agreed she would be welcome to stay with us until Easter. She agreed to move in the next day.

Roy, who knew what he was talking about, advised us to pray with her, and recommended the prayer that Pope Leo XIII had written for use wherever action of the evil one was suspected. Before she arrived, I set up a prayer table with a crucifix, holy water and a blessed candle in a red glass vigil light holder. The blessing prayer from the Roman Ritual states, "May all evil fancies of the foul fiend, his malice and cunning, be driven afar from the place where this water is sprinkled." The blessing for candles asks, "Let the blessing they receive from the sign of the Holy Cross be so effectual that wherever they are lighted or placed, the princes of darkness may depart in trembling from all these places, and flee in fear." I figured that from what Roy had told me, I would probably need both.

Roy, Dick, and I stood behind her as she kept her eyes on the crucifix, and together we recited Pope Leo's prayer aloud. As we said the last words of the prayer, the glass containing the blessed candle made a loud "PING", then shattered over the table and the floor around it. We looked at each other, and I wondered, "What on earth have we agreed to do?" I almost changed my mind. Spiritual warfare was not my choice of activities. The next nine months might be really difficult.

The next day she asked if we could clean out her apartment. "Bring your holy water and your blessing prayers. I've done some very evil things in that apartment that I am now ashamed of even touching. Recently I've had some bad experiences there and I wouldn't want anyone else to move in until the place has been blessed." Dick and I went with her to her apartment.

I took her at her word and didn't want to know what had happened. When we removed all her possessions, Dick sprinkled all the rooms with holy water and said the "Blessing of Homes" from the Roman Ritual.

She worked odd hours and was frequently around the house for much of the day. At times it would seem that something was beating her around. She would be sitting in a chair and her head and whole upper body would jerk to the side as though something hit her. At other times she would appear to be arguing with someone or something, telling it to leave her alone – she was through with all that. At such times I would pray, especially to St. Michael the Archangel, who scripture tells us (Rev. 12:7-12) threw (Satan) the dragon out of heaven, asking that he would defend us in battle. With prayer, everything would quiet down, and we would again experience the peace of God.

Because with prayer, things usually settled down, I became careless forgetting who and what was oppressing her. One day, after a particularly difficult day, our elderly cat, Hip-shot, acted as though he was struggling to breathe. It was a very hot, late, fall Florida day. At the time, only one room in our house, was air-conditioned. I took Hip shot in and laid him on the bed, thinking that he was perhaps over heated. An hour later, I went in to check on him. He was still struggling to breathe. Patricia came to the door and said, "Eve, do you suppose it could be something spiritual?" I said, "At this point, I'd believe almost anything." I got out the holy water bottle, sprinkled my cat, and commanded anything that was not of God to leave that creature of God. Hip-shot took a loud breath like sigh, meowed, and jumped off the bed to look for his food dish.

One day as we approached Easter and Baptism, she left her clipboard lying on the dining room table. I saw it as I walked past. It said in large print, "Peace must be awfully dull." I was angry. The peace of our house had been thoroughly disrupted for several months. I never really knew what was coming next, or what to expect at any time. There was nothing I wanted so much as a return to the peace experienced before Patricia's arrival. I confronted her about it and said, not kindly, "As soon as you are baptized, you need to find another place to stay. I need my peace and quiet back." As soon as I said it, I regretted it. It was unkind and unnecessary. I apologized and Patricia said she understood and would look for an apartment during Holy Week. I felt as though I had somehow rejected Christ. I apologized to Him, too.

I have seen Patricia several times since she was baptized. She shines with happiness. The first time was at the weekly prayer session at St. Margaret when Dick was leading the session for a friend. She brought two elderly women who had no other way of getting there. All was going well for her.

The next time I saw her was at the noon Mass at the Cathedral. I told her that I was worried about my daughter who was experimenting with drugs and the occult. She said, "Oh, Eve! Why do you worry? If God could get me, as He did, He can get anyone. He has her in the palm of His hand." I have seen her several more times, mostly at church, and she is always visibly very happy.

CHAPTER 8

Forgiveness Heals A Family

"If you forgive others their transgressions, your heavenly Father will forgive you. But if you do not forgive others, neither will your Father forgive your transgressions."

(Matthew 6:14-15)

Father David asked, "Eve, have you got room for an older couple?" I assured him that we had twin beds and there was room. "This older couple from Massachusetts came down here to find work. They brought all their savings with them, and over the last two months have spent all their money without finding jobs. They have been living in their car and now need a place to bathe and get a good night's sleep. They need a good address before anyone will hire them. I thought maybe they could use your address."

The ten-year-old Cadillac pulled into our drive, loaded down with clothes and suitcases. A distinguished looking, well-dressed woman in her late fifties was driving. Every hair was in place, and her makeup was perfectly applied. She got out, looked at me and said with much anger, "I have never been so humiliated in my life! To think that I have been reduced to accepting charity for a place to stay!"

The man with her looked a little older and seemed confused. He thanked us for letting them stay, but was unsure of just how or how much to unload the car. If I asked him a question, she answered. She gave him very little opportunity to talk. Dick and I introduced our selves and told them they were welcome. Eleanor gave us her name and introduced her husband Edwin, but she had little else to say. We showed them their rooms and helped them unload the car. We gave them a copy of the rules of the house, told them when supper would be ready and asked if they needed anything else. "No," she answered, "we will be fine. Right now we just need a little rest. It has been a very difficult day."

At supper that evening Eleanor opened up a little bit. She thanked us for providing room for them, and told some of her story. "Edwin was chief electrical engineer for the XXX Corporation in Massachusetts for twenty five years until he had to retire for health reasons three years ago. I was mainly involved in raising my daughter, Marie and helping at the church. Marie married that no good loafer that we told her she shouldn't marry - I knew he was no good - we still provided for them and put up with him. Even if we didn't like him, he was her choice of a husband. When the baby was born we saw that she had everything she needed. Then when he left her and the baby, we set her up with her own beauty shop business so that she could support both of them reasonably well. After the divorce, when she started going with that other man, she sold the beauty shop, gave us the money back, and told us she didn't want our help anymore. She wanted to take care of herself and the baby without our help, as though she would be able to do it all without us. The ingratitude of it all! She said I was too controlling. She wanted to live her own life. Well we'll let her live her own life all right. We took all of our money out of the bank and came down here to start a new life. We didn't tell her we were leaving or where we were going. Let her worry about us! It will serve her right for not appreciating all we did for her."

I didn't care to comment on her story, so I changed the subject. "A few friends of ours are coming over this evening for a prayer meeting. We would like to have you join us if you want." "It's not a charismatic prayer meeting is it?" she asked.

Yes it is. We get together once a week just to praise the Lord. We are now considering the possibility of forming a covenant community in order to better live our Christian life. You are welcome to join us if you want." I told her.

"That man, the one who convinced my daughter that she should break away from us, was someone she met at a charismatic prayer meeting. I wouldn't have anything to do with something that could break up a family that way. How could you be involved with something that wrong?" she asked.

I assured her that it wasn't the charismatic movement that had injured her family. "The charismatic movement does more to bring families together than it does to tear them apart. It was responsible for mending our marriage by making us both more conscious of what was God's will and what was our will. It really helped."

Later as we were washing dishes, I told her a little about our daughter and how we were separated by the difference between what she wanted and what we wanted. I told her that we couldn't approve of our daughter's choices of the occult and drugs, but God always allows us to use our free will. Her choices had many bitter consequences for us as well as for her. We couldn't allow such things into our house, but we loved her and had forgiven her the things she had done against us. I have assured my daughter, that if she ever changed her mind, we would welcome her back with open arms. "The important thing, Eleanor, is that you forgive. Forgiveness opens many doors that anger and bitterness shut tight. Unforgiveness does more harm to the person who refuses to forgive than it does to the person who isn't forgiven. Unforgiveness prevents God's action in your lives. How can He help you if you haven't forgiven your daughter? Unforgiveness like any other serious sin prevents God from giving us the help we need. We always have to leave the door open for communication."

She had no response to my story. I didn't know if she would be able to make the connection from our problems to hers. The basis of the problem was the same. You have to forgive those who hurt you, or you end up carrying the hurt like baggage. It wears you out and ruins relationships. It can even make you physically sick. I hoped she had heard what I said.

She spent most of the next three days job-hunting, and we had little time for talk. Edwin, I believed, had the beginnings of Alzheimer's or some other dementing illness. At times we could talk easily, at other times he seemed far, far away. Most of the time, while Eleanor was out looking for work, Edwin sat and stared at the walls. Either he was suffering from severe depression or was ill.

At the end of the third day of an apparently futile job search, Eleanor said, "I've been thinking. What you said about forgiveness is probably true. I've been thinking about my daughter and the argument we had. I know I need to call her, but I don't know what to say. Maybe she doesn't want to speak to me again."

"Let's say a prayer of forgiveness for her, and ask God to give you the words to say to her. I'm sure you love each other very much. She'll be very glad to hear from you and to know that you're all right. She'll need to forgive you, too, for leaving without telling her where you were going, and for making her feel that you were trying to control her life. God is rich in mercy, and He can give both of you the forgiveness you need for each other, if you'll only ask Him for it."

We prayed together as the tears rolled down her cheeks. She called her daughter later that evening, and they both cried over the phone. Edwin also talked to his daughter and for the first time since their arrival, I saw him smile.

Early the next morning she received three phone calls with offers of jobs. She took the one that offered a place to live as well as a salary for both of them. It was as live-in caretakers for an older adult communal living facility. She would keep house, do the laundry, do the shopping, cook meals and Edwin would care for the yard and do minor repair work, jobs that he could handle in spite of any incapacity he might have. It seemed so perfect as it answered all their immediate needs for a place to live as well as an income. They would start the first of the next week.

A few weeks later, she invited us to the house for dinner. Both she and Edwin seemed very satisfied with what they were doing. She told me that they were saving most of their salaries, and when they had enough saved, they were returning to Massachusetts. Her daughter wanted them to come home, and she was sure that she wouldn't make the mistake of trying to control her daughter's life again. She thanked us for our help, and especially for teaching her about the necessity of forgiving others. Her life was back on track again.

Through Eleanor and Edwin we learned again how refusal to forgive others for offending us is able to prevent God's action or help in our lives. Not only can God not forgive us if we don't forgive others, but neither can He answer our needs unless we forgive. The quick answer to all their prayers for a job after they forgave their daughter shows the power there is when we decide to forgive others as God forgives us.

CHAPTER 9

Rebellion Can Destroy A Life

"The hot-head provokes disputes, someone in a rage commits all sorts of sins."

(Proverbs 29:22)

I was weeding the garden along our driveway when a motor scooter, ridden by a boy who looked to be about fourteen years old - blonde and blue eyed, with a very winning smile, pulled noisily into our driveway. "Hi! How are you today?" he asked. "Father David told me to come and see you, that maybe you might be able to give me a room for a short while."

I answered, "Well, we might. What's your name and where are you from?"

"I come from New Jersey. My name is Jim Davis."

"How did you get here from New Jersey? That's a pretty long distance away."

"I rode my motor scooter all the way. It only took me five days."

"Where did you eat and sleep on your way down?"

"I begged food, lots of people will help a kid out. The weather was good so I slept in fields or barns along the way."

"I'll have to have your parent's name and phone number. You can't stay here without their permission. How old are you, anyway?"

"Well, I can give you my dad's name and number, but it won't matter. They threw me out last week and told me never to come back. I'm seventeen. I'll be eighteen next month. Everyone calls me the 'Munchkin' because I'm small for my age, but I can work, I can do about anything I set my mind to."

"If you're going to live on your own and not finish school and have no support from your parents, you'll have to get a job and work. Anything we can give you is only temporary. You would have to apologize for whatever made your parents so angry, and do what they told you.   If you plan to finish school so you could get a really good job, you will have to start right away and work hard.   I can't promise you anything until my husband comes home and we talk it over. Have you had anything to eat today?"

"No. I am kind of hungry."

"Well, come into the house and I'll fix you something to eat. By the time you finish, my husband should be home and we can decide what to do about you then. As I said, we'll have to call your parents before we really make any decisions. Park your scooter around the back so it won't get stolen, then come and eat."

When Dick came home, we talked about the problem of Jim Davis, and decided, maybe we might be able to help him. I called his home, his father answered. I asked him if he wanted to talk to his son, and he said "No." We told him that his son told us he was seventeen, almost eighteen, but he didn't look that old. What was his age? He was indeed seventeen. They were through with him and never wanted to see him or speak to him again.

He didn't tell me anything about what the problem was. I asked Jim and he said that when he got angry, he had "fits." I asked if he was an epileptic, and he said, "Oh, no, no! Nothing like that." I had second thoughts about whether we could handle a person with that problem, but Dick said, "He's just a kid. It can't be too bad. Maybe it's just a home problem, and he won't have it here."

We showed him his room, collected his clothes for laundry, and he began his stay with us.

We talked about what he could do to earn some money. He said that he was really good with computers, but he couldn't stand to work in an office. He couldn't sit still that long. We asked him what he would rather do, and he said he wanted to go into the service. What service was he interested in? Only the Navy. We took him to the Naval Recruiting Office, let him out, and told him to call when he was ready to come back.

We talked about the interview when he came home. They wanted him to go to a psychiatrist, to see if the doctor really thought he would be fit for the Navy and what exactly were the "fits" that he kept talking about. It seems that they gave him an intelligence test and he scored right at the top of it. That and the demonstration of his computer skills would make him a very valuable member of the Navy. If he passed the psychiatric exam, they would be willing to make an exception to their requirement for a high school diploma or a GED and the navy would take him into the service. I also learned that his "fits" were outbursts of rage when he was angered by anything. I gathered that was the reason his family forbade him from coming home again.

He spoke at length of his family. I gathered that his dad was often away and his mother was completely unable to control him. In his view, his younger brother, who was mild mannered and obedient, got all of her attention. He was told to spend most of his time in his room. In that room he had a television, a lot of video games, a computer, a cell phone, and any other electronic toys that were available at that time. In his room he had every possible distraction and mentally stimulating toy, everything except love and attention from his parents. Often they wouldn't even speak to him. He said that his mother only had one son and it wasn't him.

There were things that he needed, and, mostly for his education in the ways of the world, we told him that his food, water, and electricity cost us about $25 a week. He wouldn't be using his moped in the navy. He needed to sell it and use the money to get what he needed, and if he saw fit, to pay our expenses for keeping him. The moped sold quickly, and he did pay what he owed us. While with us he had a few of his "fits". He had broken a couple of garden tools and a few things in the house, but basically he was able to keep himself mostly under control.

When the time came for him to leave for boot camp, He said to me, " I've been thrown out of my own home, three boarding schools, five foster homes and two schools. This is the first place I've been able to stay until it's time to leave. Thanks for putting up with me." I heard from him off and on as he went through boot camp. When he graduated, his mother, dad and brother came to his graduation. He had passed his GRE exam, had his high school credit and was to be stationed on a destroyer. I thought that he was home free and thanked and praised the Lord for helping him through it. He was really on his way to a better life.

I didn't hear from him again for twelve years. It was a letter from a prison in Arizona. He asked if I could possibly send him a few dollars to buy soap, toothbrush and toothpaste, a razor and shaving cream, as he would be there for five to eight years, and they didn't provide very good things for personal cleanliness.

I asked him what happened. I was so sure he would do well for the rest of his life, that he had learned his lessons well. It seems that he had been accused of stealing a computer from his ship when it was in Hawaii. He refused to go to trial and ran to the mainland. That meant he was convicted of the crime and was wanted for prison back in Hawaii. He was speeding through Arizona, and when stopped by a State Trooper, fought him and resisted arrest. He received five to ten years for evading arrest with violence, which cost him five to eight years in prison. When he finished his full sentence with many days in solitary confinement for refusing to cooperate, he had to go to Hawaii to serve his five- year sentence there.

Several years later, he had completed all his sentences and was released with five years probation in Hawaii, but the next week he showed up on our porch in Florida. He was a bit taller. More mature, but still thin and small for a grown man. I told him he needed to turn himself in, but he was sure he knew best and said he would work for a contractor - they didn't check Social security cards or other identification.

When I told him that we lived in a neighborhood watch area, and if he stayed here, the police would probably check him out. He was furious and told me that he was leaving, otherwise he might do something he would really regret, that I had no business warning him about police checks. He was going and would never come back.

I think his decision to leave at that time, was part of God's protection for us. I don't know what he might have done to us if he had stayed at that time. Wherever he went, I know that he couldn't get a legitimate job because as soon as he gave his social security number to anyone, his unfinished parole violation would show up and he would be returned to the prison in Hawaii. I didn't hear from him for several years. I thought, maybe he's back in prison; maybe he's still running.

A few years later, I got a call from him. He was working on a job that required traveling through the south. He enjoyed his job.

A few years after that, there was a note left on my front door while I was shopping. It read, "Mom, I've got my life straightened out, and am doing well: all because of you and your house." signed, Jim Davis

Thank you, God, for rescuing that young man.

CHAPTER 10

Sister Clarice, a Very Special gift of God.

"You are God's chosen race, His saint's; He loves you."
(Colossians 3:12)

Mrs. Howell was dead. She had died in a nursing home that she hated, but could no longer take care of herself. She lived next door to us, had lived in that home since it was built in 1926. Her husband had died there while she was at his side. Her baby daughter had also died there. She had no family left, and willed the house to the Cathedral to use as they saw fit. Father David decided that the house would be a good staff house, which was needed because at that time there was a shortage of rental homes, and what was available was very expensive.

The first residents were the youth minister and his family. They stayed until they moved to Washington State. The next person to move in next door was Sister Clarice who was the new Director of Spiritual Development. She hadn't lived by herself since entering the convent years before. I became her main resource for the many problems encountered when learning to live by your self. She was getting comfortable with her new lifestyle, when the cathedral announced that it planned to sell the property. They needed the money for some new programs they planned to start. Sister Clarice was out of a job, out of a home, and out of luck. She couldn't find a rental that she could afford.

As Sister Clarice was such a gift from God, I knew that I was the one who would profit most if she came to live in God's House. I could profit from her spiritual knowledge, and would gladly make her as comfortable as possible. I learned more about spirituality from her than I had ever learned from anyone else. I was able to attend all of the workshops that she provided for the Cathedral.

Her order told her that she would have to get a private apartment. Living with a family was not compatible with the rules of her order. She got a job with the Orange County Schools teaching special home-bound high school students. She was assigned to a group of high school students who were infected with Aids. They lived in an old unused hospital where they received the treatment they needed. They went home on the weekend and many bragged about how many new cases of Aids they had started over the week end. She taught other home bound students as well. Her salary from the school board was more than what she was paid at the cathedral. So much more that she was able to support 12 other sisters in her home convent.

We continued the relationship we had established. We visited frequently, until she was diagnosed with bone cancer. We visited while she was still in the hospital. She began to lose her hair, and rapidly lost her strength. She had to return to her home convent. She took with her a sunset painting I had done while camping on the Suwanee River, and gave it to her. She had it hung over her bed, and considered it a painting of the end of life as also the end of day. She wrote that it was a great comfort for her as she faced the end of her own days. When they notified me of her death, they asked if they could keep the painting as it had meant so much to her, and they had a place where they wanted to hang it. I told them that I was glad that they wanted to keep it. They had just the place they wanted to hang it. As far as I know, it is still there.

CHAPTER 11

A Battered Wife Cannot Always Escape

"Husbands love your wives and treat them with gentleness."

(Colossians 3:19)

The call came from the social worker at the Regional Hospital. There was a badly burned woman who had been through the worst of the treatment for burns, but was homeless and needed a home to finish her recovery. They could find no other place willing to continue her minimum care. Father David had suggested they call us. As we had no other visitors, and the hospital would provide any in-home-care that she needed, we agreed to take her into our house. She also had a twelve-year-old son and a husband who could not assist in her care, and had no residence for her. They were all homeless. We told them that the son and the woman could stay with us, but we didn't have room for the husband.

They all came, and we told the husband he could visit, but would need to stay at the homeless shelter or the Salvation Army residence. After the husband had left and the son was watching television, Sheila and I had a chance to talk. Her burns, all over her chest and upper arms, were caused by her husband pouring a pot of boiling coffee over her as she laid in bed. It seems she didn't get up as soon as he thought she should get up. She was missing most of her teeth, from abuse and carried many scars, including emotional and physical scars. I asked why she still was with him, why hadn't she charged him with such abuse to the police. Such treatment was definitely illegal. He should be in prison, not walking the streets. She said, "When he is good, he is very good and because of that she still loved him." As I had a wonderful, gentle husband, I couldn't understand why she endured such use. The law was on her side and would take care of the situation, but she wouldn't prefer charges. Her husband came to visit the next day, but decided that he didn't like the feelings he got at our house and did not come back again. He phoned her regularly and she told me that he just didn't feel comfortable at our house. That pleased me very much because I didn't feel comfortable around him either.

When she was well enough to take care of herself and do the things required for comfort she would no longer need a nurse .The nurse from the hospital changed her dressings and took care of medical needs. She improved quickly. I begin to talk to her about being on her own and caring for herself and her son. We helped her find a job at a small, out of the way restaurant where she could make enough to support herself and her son. We also helped her find a furnished room where she and her son could live within her means. I just told her husband that she had left. No, I answered, I didn't know where he could find her. I really didn't know exactly where she would be at any given time. We visited her occasionally, and she was doing well. One day, when we went to the restaurant to check on how well she was doing, she wasn't there. The owner told me that her husband came into the restaurant and she left with him. She didn't even wait for the rest of the pay she had earned. He was left short a waitress.

Everyone has free will and unless they really want to escape a bad situation, no one can help them find another way. I never saw her again.

CHAPTER 12

From Near Abortion to Life

"Like a child comforted by its mother, so will I comfort you."

(Isaiah 66: 13)

She was very tall, very dark, and very pregnant. She had been staying at a battered women's shelter. They didn't have facilities for very pregnant women. The Church had referred her to us, not having other facilities for women who avoided abortion. She had three teenage daughters who were with her mother. She had left an abusive husband in New York to start a new life in Orlando, when she found she was pregnant. She had planned to find a job, save money and pay to bring her daughters to Orlando. With pregnancy, all those plans were down the drain- couldn't be done. She decided that the only logical thing would be an abortion so she could get on with her life.

At the abortion clinic, they did a sonogram to learn if there was any problem with an abortion. She watched the sonogram and saw the baby within, move and realized that it was alive, not just the cluster of cells claimed by the officials at the facility. She couldn't kill her baby. Its daddy may not be much good, but it was a baby, alive and growing. She left the clinic and went to an abused women's shelter. They called the church and were referred to us. She was about six or seven months along.

First, we put her in contact with the JMJ center in town. They provided a wardrobe and supplies for a newborn. They also helped make arrangements for hospital delivery. She helped me around the house until labor began. My husband, a much shorter, heavy-set white man was elected to drive her to the hospital. When he came home, he laughingly told of the drive. Every time a contraction came she would groan and he would say, "Not yet, hold on! Not in my car! I wouldn't know what to do! We're almost there."

He also said that when he went with her to check in, he got some mighty strange looks from the hospital staff as she registered. When the hospital staff took over, he came home, very relieved that it was over. She had a seven- pound healthy baby boy.

Fifteen years later we received a wedding invitation from her. At first I couldn't figure who she was, I had forgotten her name. When it came back, we accepted the invitation. She had found a man who appreciated her many good points and strengths. At the reception at her house, her mother and children were all there. Her fifteen-year-old-son had grown tall and handsome; her daughters had families of their own. We were seated and treated like royalty because we had helped her so long ago. It was a joyful and satisfying occasion. When you give someone assistance, you never know where it will lead. Most of the time, I never knew what happened. It was so good to learn that this time our hospitality bore very good fruit.

CHAPTER 13

Day Labor Can Be a Trap

"He said to them, "You too, go into my vineyard, and I will give you what is just."

(Mat.20: 4)

A burly, very strong looking man began attending our prayer meeting regularly. I asked him to introduce himself to our attendees. He said his name was Ted Johnson. He offered no further information, and after everyone left, I asked where he was staying.

"At the Salvation Army. It's all I can afford right now."

I asked, "Where are you working?"

"Right now, I'm doing day work. A bus pick's you up and brings you home. You have to pay for the ride both ways. Then you have to pay for your meals and your room at the Army facilities. That takes just about all you earn on a day job–it's rather a trap."

I agreed.

After a few more weeks at the prayer meeting, I suggested he come and stay at our house. Then he could save enough to pay for a better place to stay, or look for another job. He gladly came to stay with us. After a couple of weeks he went job hunting. One day, he just didn't come back. I assumed he had indeed found a job and was on his way.

A few years later, an 18-wheeler pulled up in front of our house one morning. The driver came to our door. The driver was Ted. He had joined a trucking company as a driver. He had been all over the U.S. Since we last saw him. He said he had come to take us to breakfast, before he went on the road, again. At breakfast he told us all his adventures since we last saw him. He liked his job and had been all over the U, S, , He had met many interesting people, and planned to continue working for the trucking company until he had saved enough to retire. He stopped by once more before he left, he thanked us for helping get him on his own, then went off in his big truck.

We never saw him again. He was ambitious and intelligent. I'm sure that if he isn't driving anymore, he's probably working for the company, possibly in an administrative position. As a teacher I usually can recognize talent and intelligence. I am sure if he so desired, he could still be driving that big-rig. If not, he was probably still working for the company, possibly as one of the administrators of the company.

CHAPTER 14

"A Man Can Lose His Way When He Seeks Holiness"
(I Corinthians 13:1)

The receptionist from our church called and asked if I could rent a room to a former Brother from The Order of Our Savior. He had left the order, but needed a place to stay. I told her we didn't rent rooms, but he could stay for a short while until he found something better for him. He came over to see the room and I told him that if he wanted to pay for his food and utilities, he could pay $25 a week, which should cover our expenses. The cost was agreeable, He moved in the next day.

Brother John was a huge man; very tall and so obese, he could hardly walk. He was probably in his 60's and did very little except lay on the couch, eat and watch television. Occasionally he would go out for several hours and then be very smug when he came back. He told my husband that he was baptizing homeless people downtown. God only knows if he was telling the truth. If so, he was going completely against Catholic law and teaching. Baptism requires extensive classes so that the person being baptized understands what the Church teaches and believes. It requires a recitation and agreement with the creed that states the person's belief in Jesus and agreement with the teachings of the Church

He put up all kinds of holy pictures, particularly ones of "Our Lady of Perpetual Help" and the "Sacred Heart of Jesus". He kept a lighted candle in front of each picture, which worried me very much. Our house is old, built of pitch pine and cypress, and would go up in flames in a minute with any carelessness. I asked him to be sure he put the candles out when he went to sleep, or went out of the house. I might as well have held my tongue, because he ignored my request.

He was a Vietnam war veteran, a captain, and had been a prisoner of war. He said the Vietnamese tortured all their prisoners. Because of this, he hated all Vietnamese. He always referred to them as "Gooks". That caused major problems, because our church was shared with a Vietnamese parish. Father Nguyen worked with all the masses and parishioners as assistant to own pastor.

Father Nguyen was much loved by our parish because he was always cheerful and friendly to every one. Brother John made his dislike felt from the beginning. His experience of torture might explain part of his unpleasant manners, but really didn't excuse them. I suggested that he try to forgive those who had kept him prisoner. "I'll never forgive those *^##*#! animals-NEVER!" I said, "Then how do you expect to be forgiven? We pray in the Our Father, forgive us our sins as we forgive those who sin against us. Forgiveness is not an option it is a requirement." He turned and walked away.

I thought I had made it plain that I would do the cooking, But the next day, he went to the grocery and brought home all kinds of things that we did not eat such as fatty snack food and all kinds of fatty eats and sugary deserts. He brought home so much junk food that he filled up the refrigerator and buried the food that I would serve under it. I explained that anything in the refrigerator or cupboards in the kitchen was for all persons in the house, but in order for me to know what was available for meals, I would need to know when he used anything that he had not purchased. My refrigerator was no longer mine. He had taken it over. I told him that the kitchen was out of bounds for him, and asked would he please remove anything that did not require refrigeration so I would have access to our food. Very grudgingly he took out the beer, the snacks and other non-essentials, and pouted for the rest of the day. As the week wore on he complained about everything. He didn't like the way I fixed potatoes. They were not crisp, because they had not been deep-fried. The rice I prepared was brown rice, which, for health reasons, we use exclusively. He said that it wasn't rice, it was the same crap that they fed him in the prison in Vietnam. He didn't eat vegetables, just meat and starch. Since he didn't want anything I cooked, I told him that he had better eat elsewhere in a place that pleased his tastes. My patience was about gone and I told him that since he was so unhappy with everything, he also needed to look for a better place to stay. He made no effort to find any other place.

My husband and I decided we would go canoeing on the beautiful Wekiva River, to get away from the tensions he brought into our house. We told Brother John we would be back before dinner. It was a beautiful Florida day, bright sun and not too hot, so we packed a picnic lunch, loaded the canoe on the car, and left.

We unloaded the canoe, put our lunch and gear into it, then realized that we had forgotten our paddles. You can't go far without paddles. We put the lunch and gear back into the car, asked the ranger if we could leave the canoe on the beach. He said he would watch it until we came back. As we pulled into our home driveway, a boy, no older than 14-15, came out of our house and ran down the driveway. I asked him what he was doing in our house and why was he there. He said he was a friend of John's and had been visiting. I rushed into the house, and Brother John was half undressed, the bedroom was a mess, and I realized that the boy was probably one of the street male prostitutes who walked a downtown park. It was common knowledge that anyone who was interested could get what ever they wanted for a price. When I asked Brother John what was going on, he told me that what he did while we were gone was none of our business. My husband told him to get all of his things and leave. We would wait until he was gone and lock the door behind him. Such activities were immoral and illegal. He collected his few belongings and left. Several years later when the child molestation scandal broke in the church, I knew why Brother John would not go to his religious order for help in getting settled, and why he had been thrown out of that Order. I also understood why he could not return. Sexual molestation of those under eighteen is a despicable crime. May God have mercy on him. I learned that the vows of poverty chastity and obedience did not mean that the person was honoring those vows. Again I learned that if we were going to continue with our ministry, we had to pray for discernment before we accepted anyone into our home.

We never heard from Brother John again. We have seen him around town, mostly in grocery or convenience stores, buying snack foods and cigarettes. He never acknowledged that he has seen or knows who we are, and we do the same. No one, even a child molester is exempt from God's mercy. We also ask that God have mercy on him. No one but God knows what he went through in Vietnam, or if his experiences there robbed him of his sanity, or destroyed his ability to think. Only God can judge him with justice, mercy, and truth. Perhaps someday we will meet him in heaven. Only God knows.

CHAPTER 15

God Guides Those He Loves

"Whether I walk or lie down you are watching. You know every detail of my conduct."

(Psalm 139: 3)

A woman's voice on the other end of the phone said, "This is Deputy Kelly of the Duval County Sheriff's Department. Is this Mrs. Rupp?" My mind began to race. The only people we knew in Jacksonville, (Duval County), were my sister and brother-in-law and their family. I was sure some catastrophe had happened to them, and that's why the sheriff's department was calling. I answered, "Yes, this is Mrs. Rupp. How can I help you?" Deputy Kelly said, "I have an African religious woman here. She wants to stay a week at your mission." I told her, "We don't have a mission. We have a private home that we sometimes allow people to stay in for short periods. We usually have a priest or social worker check them out before they come. Let me give you the number of the diocese African/ Haitian mission. Speak to Father Rudy there. If he recommends that we take this woman in, we'll gladly welcome her."

She thanked me and ended the conversation. I thought that everything had been taken care of, and if Father Rudy didn't call, that was the end of that. The next day I heard a car in our drive and when I went to look, it was a taxicab. The driver was helping a woman in a nun's habit out of the cab, suitcase and all. She introduced herself and said that her name was Sister Mary Clare, and she was from Zimbabwe, Africa. As I was no longer familiar with the new geography of Africa, I asked if that was the country that used to be Rhodesia. She assured me, in a very refined English accent, that it was. She told me that she was on sabbatical and was touring the United States. She had always wanted to see Disney World, and Sea World. She had money for the parks, but could not afford both the park entrance fees and a place to stay.

I welcomed her and made her as comfortable as I could, and let her settle into our spare room. She was a member of a woman's religious order in the Episcopal Church in Zimbabwe. She taught in one of the religious elementary schools there. She had visited the mother house of her order in Georgia before coming to Florida.

I offered to take her to Disney, as we have free passes because my husband had worked there for twenty-three years, but I couldn't take her to the other parks.

She said "Thank you, but no. I would rather visit by myself." I told her we would have supper for her when she returned. She thanked me and said that she would rather eat at the parks she visited. Pleading exhaustion, she retired for the night.

She was up early the next morning. After the skimpiest breakfast, walked to the bus stop. We didn't hear from her until she arrived home late in the evening. I asked questions about her home and job in Africa, but beyond introductions and greetings, she wasn't very facile in English and wasn't very interested in much conversation. I learned a little about her country, but not any more than simple answers to my questions. I suspect that American English wasn't comfortable for her with her combination of African and English accents.

On her third day with us, I told her that the space shuttle would be taking off that evening, and we could see it from the lake a few blocks from us. She was very interested and that evening we drove to a bridge over a nearby lake. We listened to the radio to know when the shuttle was launched, and then we saw it. The entire Eastern sky lit up in bright red, and the white light of the shuttle streaked toward the sky. It was an exciting moment.

The next morning the newspaper was filled with pictures and articles about the launch. I gave her the paper to take back to Zimbabwe with her. She thanked us and went back to her school in Zimbabwe.

I have no idea at all how she got our phone number, or found her way to our house. For me it was one of God's mysteries. The only way I can imagine that she found us is that God guided her there. Since all the troubles in the civil war in Zimbabwe, I wonder how she is getting along. We never heard from her again, and don't know if she is home with God or still suffering the effects of that terrible war.

CHAPTER 16

A Very Special Gift: The Vocation To Be A Deacon

"For many are called but few are chosen."
(Matthew 22:14)

Dick and I were preparing for a week's camping trip to our property on the Suwanee River in North Florida. Collecting all the gear, food, and clothing for a week in the wilderness took a lot of planning and packing took quite a bit of time. While we were in the process, we received a visit from the seminarian that was visiting our church on vacation. We told him what we were doing. He asked us to pray for him as he was having doubts about his vocation to the priesthood. We told him where we were going and invited him to join us. We explained that our campsite on the river was a wonderful place for prayer, because of the beauty of the spot and the silence. There were no sounds but those of nature.

He agreed that it would be a good place for prayer, and would enjoy coming with us. We told him what to bring for himself for a week and he went back to the rectory to pack.

After setting up camp, and having dinner, we had time for all of us to pray. The silence and the beauty made God seem very close. The week, with fishing, hiking, canoeing, watching the wildlife and prayer time went very quickly. There was always something to do. At the end of the week we asked if he had received his answer. He assured us he had, but didn't share what he had decided.

After packing up and returning to Orlando, I asked Dick how his week had gone. He got a very puzzled look on his face and said yes, it had gone very well. I asked if he knew what the answer was for the seminarian. He answered, "No, but I received an answer for myself." I asked what it was and he changed the subject. Only after a conversation with Father David did he tell me he had heard his call to become a deacon.

To become a deacon in the Catholic Church is not easy. It requires not only three years of Pastoral Ministry classes for both of us, but also three years of classes in the studies and duties of a Deacon for both of us. The church wisely requires that wives understand what their husband's duties will be. At the end of Pastoral Ministry training we were both commissioned as Pastoral Ministers in the church. That meant that we promised to serve the church, mostly in one category. I promised to serve the poor and homeless. We agreed to three more years of training for Dick to become a deacon. As a deacon, he would assist the priest as educator, minister to the aged and poor, at liturgies, and with preaching.

Our ministry with God's House would continue as it had been, but with the additional duties of a deacon. Dick was a very good homilist (preacher). He also served the sick in the senior residences and the hospitals, bringing them the Word of God and communion. He was a deacon, working every day for eleven years, when his health failed. I never knew him to be more happy and fulfilled than he was as a deacon.

He was giving out communion at Mass when he collapsed on the altar steps. He insisted that he could drive himself home, but when he got there, he was unable to get out of the car. I called the emergency squad who took him to the hospital where he was immediately placed in intensive care.

He had been a machinist all his working life. He didn't like and would never use a respiratory mask, which meant that during the Vietnam War while machining explosives, he inhaled the dust from them. When working for Disney for 23 years, he machined and inhaled many dangerous materials including fiberglass, insulation and other dangerous materials. He had smoked cigarettes for many years, quitting just before we started pastoral ministries training. His lungs were destroyed. He couldn't absorb enough oxygen to live. He refused to stay in the hospital, but wanted to come home.

I called the Hospice of the Comforter. They brought in a hospital bed and oxygen tanks and made him as comfortable as possible. A nurse stayed with him 24 hours a day.

On his last morning, I woke up to the sound of him joking and laughing with the nurse. I thought, "Good, he's feeling better." The nurse agreed, thought he no longer needed 24 hour care and was preparing to leave, when he coughed very hard. He coughed up what appeared to be a piece of his lung, and went into a coma. The nurse stayed. I sat beside him with my arm around his chest when suddenly he opened his eyes wider than I had ever seen them. He looked at the ceiling and got the most joyful expression on his face, then he was gone. I think I watched him go to heaven.

CHAPTER 17

God's Concern For Widows

"The Real Widow who is all alone has set her hope on God and continues in supplication and prayers night and day."

(Timothy 5:5)

Never have I experienced such pain as the pain of widowhood. It made me realize how little I recognized what my mother went through when my father died. I am still, at times, overcome with mourning and tears. I thought after three months my mother should have been ready for other activities, and I was encouraging her to get involved with church organizations and ministry to keep her busy. I now know it was too much, too soon.

Being alone in that large house was one of the most unpleasant things I had ever experienced. I was not afraid. I knew that God took care of me. But, after 56 years of marriage, having no one to talk to, no one to help with repairs, or ask for advice was difficult. Besides those difficulties the loneliness and silence was overwhelming. I kept the TV on just to hide the silence.

I had asked my unmarried daughter to come and stay with me. She had been laid off after 20 years as a Microbiologist at the University. They closed their research department and laid off many workers and professors.

There was no chance of her finding a job near her home in Northern Florida. I thought she might be able to find a job in Central Florida, or, if she got certified as a Medical Technologist, she could get a job at any hospital. All the businesses around her home told her she was overqualified for employment. He brother asked her to come to North Carolina and find a job at a University there; She refused both offers and would not leave her beautiful, riverfront home. I had no one to stay with me.

One evening, the front door knocker sounded. When I answered the door there was a young man standing there. "Do you remember me" he asked. I answered truthfully that I didn't. "I'm Donald Jones, I stayed several months with you when I was 17," I still didn't remember him, but I invited him in and I asked what he had been doing since he left. He told me that he was employed at a nearby grocery chain store. His job was commodity control, keeping the shelves stocked and handling all incoming stock. He said that he had been through 4 years of Methodist seminary, but had not been ordained.

He had been at Dick's funeral, and still remembered his time with us. I asked if he had a place to stay. He had a room and a cleaning responsibility at one of the downtown churches. I asked if he would like to use our front bedroom. He agreed that would be a good idea. He moved in the next day. I was very glad to have someone I had known be company in my silent house. We had many interesting conversations. Later he told me that he believed the Lord had told him to come and take care of the widow.

My daughter didn't like him. She refused to talk to me as long as he was in my house. When she met him she said he gave her the creeps, but for me he was an answer to prayer. My daughter had been unable to find a job near her north Florida home, because so many workers and professors had been laid off when the University closed its research department. Because of the lack of jobs, if someone got funding for research, they were able to hire professors for job's like my daughter had. Other employers said that she was over qualified. When her unemployment ran out with no possible job opportunities, she sold her art glass collection and bought mainly cigarettes, and little food. She died in her sleep from a massive cerebral hemorrhage. Try as I might, I had not been able to mend our relationship, she would not even talk to me on the phone. I believe that her depression and her addiction to cigarets which I did not allow to be used in my house, caused the alienation between us.

Donald was a big help. He helped me through the additional grief of my daughter's death. He also helped with cleaning and other small chores around the house. When I fell, which was not unusual, he helped me up and did any small chore I asked of him. Most of all he was company. We had long conversations about music, television, politics, religion, and other subjects. Just the sound of someone else in the house was a comfort for me.

He stayed about a year and a half until the worst of the grieving was over. He was pleasant company and really helped with the grieving process. One night he left after I had gone to sleep. I never heard from him again. I believe he was sent by God to take care of the widow.

Chapter 18

"Joy in the Morning, Safety at Night."

(Psalms 30:5)

So how much good did we really do in our thirty-three years of welcoming strangers? I have heard of successes from a very small percentage of those we attempted to serve. There were many more, (500+) than the stories told here. These stories are all as true as I can remember, only all names have been changed. Some of the others, I know, were not helped at all, but returned to the ways that put them in trouble in the first place. I imagine that some we didn't hear from also were helped, but how much or how often I have no idea. God didn't tell us we would succeed; He only let us know that we should take in anyone He sent to us. We sincerely tried to do that. We are not responsible for success or failure. God took what we did and worked with it as He pleased. Just to see the few successes that He brought to our attention out of our stumbling efforts is one of the greatest joys of my life. Blessed be God who loves all of us sinners so much and brings such good out of our bumbling efforts that we truly have --"Joy in the morning, safety in the evening, under the shadow of God's wings."